Original title:
Life's Purpose (Currently on Pause)

Copyright © 2025 Creative Arts Management OÜ
All rights reserved.

Author: Dante Kingsley
ISBN HARDBACK: 978-1-80566-237-2
ISBN PAPERBACK: 978-1-80566-532-8

A Heart Resting on Hope

My heart took a break, went on a small trip,
Left a note saying, "Just need a sip!"

Waiting for inspiration, it ordered a soda,
While I binge on reruns of every old moda.

I check the mailbox, each day with a grin,
Hoping for letters from places I've been.

Instead, it's the bills, they won't go away,
I'll send my heart postcards—"Wish you were gay!"

Fleeting Glimmers in the Fog

In the fog, I lose sight, but what can I do?
I chase after shadows, imagining you.

They say there's a light, somewhere up ahead,
But I tripped on a squirrel, now my path's full of dread.

The glimmers flicker, like stars in the haze,
Reminding me gently, it's just one of those days.

I'll dance with the mist, make it swirl and twirl,
And laugh at the notion, that life's just a whirl!

Dreams Cradled in Stillness

In my chair, I sit, with dreams piled high,
I swear they're all snoozing, not even a sigh.

Each time I remember a goal gone awry,
I chuckle and wave like a silly goodbye.

They say patience is key; I'm locked in a room,
While cat videos blossom, I feel the bloom.

But eventually, I'll rise, like toast from a grill,
For today I'll just revel, in quiet and chill.

The Weight of Unmade Decisions

They say too much choice can make your head spin,
I stand at two doors, wondering where to begin.

One leads to adventure, the other to sleep;
I'm pulling my hair out—this decision is steep!

I could have had pizza or tried sushi rolls,
But now I'm just here, counting the holes in my soles.

I might just declare that today's a big flop,
And call it a win if I don't want to stop!

Whispers of Dreams Deferred

In the land of what could be,
Lies a sock with a degree.
It studied hard, but took a nap,
In the drawer, it's trapped in a flap.

The clock ticks on, it pulls a prank,
Watches me, then starts to stank.
I promised it a grand old show,
But all it gets is tea and woe.

The Stillness Between Beats

Time took a sip of lemonade,
Then plopped itself in a charade.
It juggles thoughts, but drops a few,
Where did that good idea stick like glue?

I tried to dance, but oh, the pause!
Tripped over dreams, what's the cause?
In this pit stop, I take a sip,
Of frozen thoughts, a comic slip.

Navigating the Lull

Sailing on a sea of sighs,
With seagulls who only tell lies.
They squawk and laugh, then take a swing,
At half-baked notions they bring.

A turtle raced the flowing tide,
But fell asleep, what a ride!
He dreamed of marathons and cheer,
While I just waited for the beer.

When Time Holds Its Breath

Time's on a break, just chillin' out,
While I'm here pacing about.
It forgot its watch on the couch,
And now I'm stuck, like a slouch.

An ant is playing hide and seek,
While I await the next cheek to cheek.
A moment's pause, an awkward glance,
Is this really the time for a dance?

Murmurs of Hope

In the fridge, leftovers hum,
Forgotten sauces, feeling glum.
A treadmill gathers dust and sighs,
While I chase snacks, oh what a prize!

Puns and dreams wrapped in cheese,
Juggling plans like sticky bees.
Each leap of faith feels like a trip,
As I navigate this coffee sip.

I sit and ponder what to do,
Should I dance, or just nap too?
A comfort zone wrapped in a quilt,
Where ambitions fade, and hope is built.

Yet laughter echoes through these halls,
In every stumble, joy enthralls.
So here I pause, but with good cheer,
And share my musings far and near.

The Intermission of Fate

Caught in a plot with no clear cue,
I check my watch, is this déjà vu?
Life's a movie hit the brakes,
Should I snack or grab some stakes?

Popcorn's popped, but where's the show?
The credits roll, yet no one knows.
A comedy, or tragic farce,
I laugh out loud, but it's not sparse.

The cast all giggles in the wings,
As waiting feels like silly flings.
With every tick, the humor's rife,
What's next for me? A pause in life.

So I sip my drink and make a bet,
That fun will come, who knows just yet?
In this intermission, take a cue,
Life's play resumes, and laughter too.

Caught in the Tides

Waves roll in, then roll back out,
I float along, not filled with doubt.
Surfing here, in my own head,
Catching dreams like nets, instead.

The ocean sings a goofy song,
Where clams dance silly all day long.
I wonder if I should let go,
Ride the whimsy, let it flow.

Flip-flops flapping, seagulls squawk,
As I forget my morning walk.
Paddling through this wavy day,
With quirky thoughts that make me sway.

Yet each splash brings a chuckle too,
In every twist, a glimpse of blue.
I'll ride these waves, with grit and glee,
Before the tide brings back to me.

The Unwritten Chapter

My book lies open, pages bare,
With inkless pens that float in air.
This chapter pause, so warm and bright,
Turns every word into delight.

Plot twists expected, yet no cue,
Characters waiting for their due.
Should I sketch a scene of delight,
Or merely doodle through the night?

Quirky stories whisper low,
With every line, the giggles grow.
Adventures beckon, oh so near,
But I just sit with doubts and beer.

Yet as the pen begins to glide,
A little mischief sneaks inside.
In this unwritten, wacky dance,
I find my muse, and take a chance.

The Space of Waiting

In a world where plans collide,
Procrastination takes a ride.
I search for meaning in my socks,
Lost in thoughts of pizza blocks.

The clock ticks loud, it seems to mock,
As I ponder life while watching rocks.
Do I take a leap or skip the jump?
Maybe I'll nap, or eat a lump!

Starlit Paths Untraveled

Next to the stars, my dreams float high,
But my feet seem stuck, oh me, oh my!
Should I chase the moon or just lounge here?
I'll pick up snacks and sip a beer.

A map in hand but miles away,
I'll dance in circles, come what may.
Adventures pause, it's all a jest,
The couch is calling, I must invest!

When Time Takes a Breath

Time has stopped, and I can't be blamed,
For finding joy in all that's unclaimed.
I tried to jog but just sat instead,
Imagining journeys inside my head.

With ice cream in hand, I take a seat,
Wondering if frozen treats count as a feat.
While the sun winks on through the trees,
I'm stuck in a breeze, just me and the cheese!

The Heart's Interlude

My heart is on pause, taking a rest,
Like a sloth in a hammock, feeling blessed.
I'm collecting excuses like rare Pokémon,
While hoping my problems just disappear at dawn.

A laugh here, a break there, feels like a win,
With a heart full of giggles, how can I begin?
To wander is fine, to ponder is nice,
But first, let's see if there's more pizza slice!

The Weight of Unmade Decisions

I ponder choices, big and small,
Like pie vs. cake at the annual ball.
Should I choose the red or the blue?
In the end, I'll just have stew!

I stand on the fence, feeling confused,
While recommending what's been refused.
Should I dive in or just delay?
Maybe I'll nap— it's safer that way!

Procrastination is an artful no-go,
Like waiting to see if my plants will grow.
Each moment I stall feels like a trick,
Guess I'll keep spinning my own little chick!

Decision making? It's such a bore,
My couch whispers sweetly, "Just one more."
As I sit here feeling all agog,
I'll let my choices sit like a soggy dog!

Footprints in the Sand of Time

Once I walked where tides would play,
Then changed my mind— went back to stay.
My footprints washed away with a laugh,
As if the ocean knew my inner math.

I tried to step, to see what's next,
But the sand said, "Nah, you're too perplexed."
I giggled as waves danced with my shoes,
They must think I'm just a bit of a snooze.

Tides come in with plans of their own,
Whispering secrets, so fast they're gone.
I'll lie on the beach, let the sun have its say,
Shadows and footprints? Just part of the play!

Maybe tomorrow, I'll make my mark,
But today's for daydreams, a walk in the park.
So let the waves take my worries away,
And I'll build a sand castle for a rainy day!

Whispers of the Unseen

I once had a plan, it was bold and bright,
Until I tripped over my own left foot, quite a sight.
Now I sit on the couch, remote in hand,
My ambitions are napping, as I snooze on demand.

With snacks all around, my heart's in a crunch,
I ponder my dreams, while devouring my lunch.
The universe chuckles, where did I roam?
In this masterpiece of chaos, I've found my home.

Shadows Waiting for Dawn

In the morning light, I'll find my groove,
But first, I'll finish this series; don't want to move.
The coffee brews slow, my brain takes a stroll,
While my dreams are like socks, lost in a hole.

I hear the world calling, but here I remain,
With my trusty old blanket, it's all such a gain.
"Get up!" says my friend, but I just let out a sigh,
Today's mission is simple: napping, oh my!

Holding Patterns

Waiting in limbo, what's my next act?
I could chase after fortune, but oh, that's a fact.
The couch is so comfy, it hugs me so tight,
I'm mastering the art of avoiding the light.

Look out for the plan, shining like gold,
But it flickers and fades, just like tales of old.
Outside there's a world that's buzzing and bright,
Yet here in my fortress, I'm happy all night.

A Canvas Unpainted

My canvas is waiting, but I've lost the brush,
Maybe I'll paint later, perhaps in a rush.
Colors swirl in my head, like jellybeans sweet,
But first, it's time for a snack – can't skip that treat.

Thoughts dance in circles, like kids on a spree,
Imagining greatness while stuck with TV.
"Tomorrow," I promise, "I'll give it my all,"
For now, I'll just stand here, enjoying the fall.

Echoes of Unwritten Futures

In the attic of dreams, dust bunnies play,
Wearing hats of ambition, they sway all day.
They whisper of journeys, yet to unfold,
While I sit with my snacks, feeling quite bold.

Calendars flip like a fish on a line,
Every day feels like a slow-moving vine.
Plans doing the cha-cha, never quite set,
But I'm caught in this dance, with no need to fret.

Pausing at the Crossroads

Two signs point left, one says 'Go away!',
The other insists, 'Stay for ice cream today!'
I scratch my head, but my tummy knows best,
So I ditch my own path, and head for the rest.

Do I launch or just lounge, it's such a tough choice,
In a world full of noise, I'll silence my voice.
A chair and a snack, that's the plan I decree,
Maybe tomorrow, I'll start being me.

Moments of Reflection

Staring at my mirror, who's that I see?
A sleepy old sloth who drinks lots of tea.
With thoughts full of grandeur, and plans made of fluff,
I ponder my future, while munching on stuff.

The clocks tick away like they're in a race,
But I'm glued to my couch, what a lovely place!
The curtains are drawn, the popcorn is popped,
In the kingdom of leisure, I shall never stop.

Beneath the Surface of Still Waters

Ripples of thought in a pond deep and wide,
A fish with a fedora comes in for a ride.
With each splash of insight, I giggle and grin,
As the bubbles of wisdom escape from within.

The lilies are laughing, they dance on their stems,
While I ponder my options, like choosing new gems.
So I float with the breeze and let worries flee,
For the world can wait, when you've got tea and glee.

Silent Conversations with Tomorrow

I chat with the future, it chuckles back,
Its diary's blank, just a little bit slack.
We toss ideas like a game of catch,
But all it throws are thoughts that scratch.

I ask for a sneak peek, it looks away,
It's busy daydreaming, come what may.
With popcorn thoughts, we laugh and sigh,
Waiting for answers that seem to fly.

In the Quiet of Waiting

I sit in silence, a chair made of dreams,
Counting the sandwiches, or so it seems.
The clock spins stories, tick-tock, who cares?
I think of the snacks and forget my repairs.

A parade of thoughts marches through my mind,
With costumes of hope, both silly and blind.
They trip on ideals, tumble on fears,
But giggle and wiggle through laughter and tears.

Latent Aspirations

I've buried goals in a blanket so tight,
Like lost socks hiding in the depths of night.
They whisper sweet nothings, 'Come out, oh please!'
But comfort and cheese are just so much ease.

A wish on a shelf, collecting some dust,
While ambition's napping, I munch on my crust.
But at least, you see, I've got a good plot,
As I ponder my future, and that pickle I bought.

Unraveled Ambitions

My dreams strut around in mismatched shoes,
They laugh at my plans like they're just old news.
They dance on my to-do list, flopping about,
Chasing away worries with their silly shout.

I once had a map, but it turned into art,
Now it decorates walls, plays a waiting part.
So here I doodle, all smiles and sighs,
While tangled up dreams wave their sleepy goodbyes.

The Silent Symphony

In the quiet of a room, I sit,
Searching for a purpose, just a bit.
But my socks are mismatched, what a view,
Maybe that's what I'm meant to do!

The cat keeps circling, on a quest,
To find my lunch, oh what a jest.
I try to focus on the grand design,
But he's got the plan, and it's just fine.

The clock ticks loud, it's on the fritz,
Counting moments like I count my hits.
"Time to get serious!" I decree,
Then trip on my shoelace, laughing with glee.

So here I am, sipping tea so slow,
Plotting my future, or just taking a show.
Maybe I'll dance, or take a nap,
Life's a circus; I'll grab my cap!

Moments Suspended in Time

Caught in the act of doing nothing,
My remote's the best, it needs no stuffing.
Channels of dreams flicker on the screen,
Oh, vibrant life! What does it mean?

I make a to-do list, it grows so bold,
Wash the dishes? Well, that's on hold.
Pasta or pizza, it's a deep debate,
Meanwhile, my laundry is having a fate.

I watch the dust bunnies dance on the floor,
They're holding a meeting, I want in for sure.
Every moment's a meeting of sorts,
Am I late or just taking reports?

Time rolls on like a ball of yarn,
Every twist and turn leaves me worn.
Yet giggles pop like bubbles in air,
In the pause, I find laughter everywhere!

A Prism of Possibilities

With every choice, a light refracts,
Potato chips or pies? Such fun impacts.
The fridge is bare, a sight to behold,
Yet snacks make my ambition bold.

Reflecting thoughts like rainbows in spray,
Should I be serious? No, not today!
The world is wide, with paths to tread,
But my couch calls me, so I'll stay instead.

I ponder deeply, but my thoughts go astray,
Should I write my novel? Or just hit replay?
The plot thickens like my morning brew,
Yet I'm still undecided on what to do.

In a world of colors, bright and loud,
I'll take a plunge without being proud.
For every detour, a new tale unfurls,
Maybe my pause is my gem in pearls!

Stirring in the Stillness

In the stillness, there's a tickle of fun,
As I stare at my plants, all is said and done.
One's growing sideways, making a show,
While I chase my dreams—where did they go?

I tried yoga, but the dog thinks it's play,
Pouncing on my mat, making chaos sway.
My zen turned to giggles, oh what a twist,
Maybe my purpose is wrapped in a list.

I find my muse in the whispers of tea,
Every sip a secret just for me.
The world outside may rush and race,
But here in my bubble, I've found my space.

So here's to the pauses, where laughter springs,
And the joy of wandering—oh, how it sings!
In the silence, I hear a delightful refrain,
Life's not a race; it's a whimsical game!

Dreams in Suspension

I had big plans to change the world,
But all I do is binge and twirl.
My vision board, now just a mess,
Stuck in a phase of cozy stress.

A mountain of laundry, dishes piled high,
I swear I'll get to them... oh my!
But Netflix keeps me on the couch,
My dreams postponed, that's the Ouch!

I once wrote goals in careful script,
Now they're lost, maybe I skipped.
My ambition floats like bubbles in air,
Popped by snacks and a comfy chair.

Yet in this stillness, there's some cheer,
I'll laugh it off with pizza here.
While visions linger in my mind,
I'll just pretend I'm in rewind.

When Tomorrow Holds Its Breath

Tomorrow whispered, 'Don't you fret,'
'Just pause your hustle, it's not a bet.'
So here I sit with coffee in hand,
While grand plans evaporate like sand.

The clock ticks slowly, it mocks my dream,
I'll get to it all—at least that's the theme.
My to-do list is now a fun game,
Finding joy in procrastination's name.

With aspirations like balloons gone awry,
I wonder if I'm a genius or sly.
As dreams float by with a wink and a grin,
I'll embrace this space where chaos can spin.

So here's to the moments of just hanging out,
Where thinking too hard is a conundrum of doubt.
Laughter and snacks, that's how we thrive,
In the pause of tomorrow, I'm truly alive.

The Pause of Becoming

In a world that spins much too fast,
I've hit the brakes, hoping this lasts.
With plans tucked away like laundry unfold,
I chuckle at futures I bought and sold.

My goals are now fuzzy, like an old screen,
I dream of glories I've never seen.
Do I really need to learn the guitar?
Or can I just be a pizza star?

Every 'later' is just a chance on repeat,
I'll dance to the rhythm of my own beat.
What's wrong with a break? I ask in delight,
This pause feels quite perfect, just need a bite.

While the clock ticks away a funny tune,
I'm the queen of this lazy afternoon.
So here's to the giggles amidst the set,
In my pause, I'm a legend you won't forget!

Eclipsing Ambitions

My dreams eclipse like the sun at noon,
Hidden behind a sleepy cartoon.
With ambitions that loom like a friendly shark,
Let's settle for snacks and a cozy park.

I had plans to conquer a mountain of fears,
But Netflix and snacks, they've won all my cheers.
As I scroll through my phone, my to-do list sleeps,
And I giggle at goals that are buried in heaps.

With visions of grandeur all gathering dust,
Who knew taking breaks could be so just?
I dance with distraction, my favorite tune,
Embracing the pause under a bright moon.

So cheers to the moments of glorious rest,
Where ambitions take coffee and chat with the best.
In this quirky eclipse, I'll laugh and unwind,
Life's wacky detours are simply divine.

A Seeker's Respite

In the quest for meaning, I take a snack,
A peanut butter sandwich, no turning back.
The universe waits, all silent and still,
Where's the GPS for my cosmic thrill?

Dancing with shadows under the moon,
At least my cat thinks it's a fun afternoon.
Meditating on naps, I ponder my fate,
While Netflix and ice cream patiently wait.

I set out to find my grand master plan,
But the couch's embrace is where I began.
With dreams like popcorn, they pop and they fly,
Yet here I am laughing without knowing why.

Navigating the Silence

In the grand scheme, I've taken a break,
Like a turtle in yoga, my mind's at stake.
Emails pile up like socks in the dryer,
While my mind's a still pond, no thoughts to inspire.

A roadmap of doodles on the coffee stain,
Now I'm a cartographer for bliss and for pain.
With coffee as fuel, I make wild decisions,
Like wearing my pajamas during all my missions.

Instead of grand changes, I'll bake a cake,
Maybe I'll call it 'The Great Pause' mistake.
With laughter as frosting, and patience as sprinkles,
I'll feast on my dreams, and dance in the wrinkles.

Hibernation of the Soul

If I had a dollar for every deep thought,
I'd have just enough to buy dreams I forgot.
Wrapped in my blanket, with tea by my side,
I ponder the mountains, but stay sweetly fried.

The squirrels outside are in quite the rush,
While I'm here wondering if I should just hush.
To sleep like a bear, to snore with intent,
Is the greatest of journeys, I truly consent.

Awakening seems like a faraway tune,
Where's my marching band? Where's my bright balloon?
For now I'll enjoy this cozy cocoon,
And skip all the quests that lead to monsoon.

The Calm Before Motion

Before the great race, I hit the snooze,
Another five minutes? Oh, what do I choose?
The world is a stage, but the curtain is drawn,
And I'm backstage laughing, still in my yawn.

Plans on a whiteboard, waiting to bloom,
Yet here I am reveling in my living room.
Why rush to the finish when the snacks are divine?
I'll conquer my hunger before I align.

With popcorn for fuel and Netflix on blast,
I'm kicking back hard; leave the work for the last.
So here's to the moments that stretch like the sun,
Where taking a break is the most splendid fun.

Inertia of the Spirit

My feet are glued to the floor,
Like I'm waiting for a score.
The couch calls out my name,
In this game, I feel no shame.

I ponder grand plans to chase,
But only find my comfy place.
Procrastination is my art,
And cheese puffs fill my heart.

I plan to run a marathon,
But there's Netflix to lean upon.
A busy day ends with a snack,
Who needs speed when you've got a nap?

Tomorrow's a word I often say,
But today? Well, let's just play.
Each moment's a dance on pause,
With smiles as my only cause.

The Garden of Tomorrow's Seeds

I planted thoughts in the soil,
But weeds of worry make it toil.
I water dreams with lazy rain,
Yet my garden feels a bit mundane.

Each blossom waits to take its chance,
But here I sit, not in a dance.
I'll start to grow—oh yes, I will!
Once I've finished this last meal.

The daisies wave, 'come play with us!'
But I'm wrapped in a cozy fuss.
I hold a shovel, muse in hand,
Yet dig a trench for dreams unplanned.

The sun peeks through, a playful tease,
While I relax beneath the trees.
Today I bloom—if just in thought,
A garden riot I've long sought.

Stasis of a Wandering Heart

My heart has packed its bags for sure,
But it's lost in a park, that's for sure.
It wanders, looks around the block,
Then settles down to play with the clock.

I'm on a journey to build a dream,
But there's a comfy chair that screams.
With every step, I check the time,
Yet end up sipping lemon-lime.

A soul in transit, a heart in pause,
Spinning in circles, what's the cause?
I map my path but take the stairs,
To Netflix corners, comfy chairs.

Let's put the plans back on the shelf,
For now I'll just enjoy myself.
Tomorrow I'll rise with purpose and zest,
Today I'll nap—this is my quest.

The Pause of a Thousand Possibilities

A thousand dreams reside in me,
But they're all on coffee breaks, you see.
I've got ambitions stacked like books,
But they hide beneath my cozy nooks.

Potential bounces like a ball,
Yet here I sit, I hardly crawl.
I toss ideas in the air,
And watch them float without a care.

Each thought's a bird ready to fly,
But first, I need that second pie.
The pause button's a charming sight,
In this moment, all feels right.

With joy, I embrace the idle pace,
With laughter, I fill each empty space.
So here I stand, arms wide and bright,
As possibilities twinkle in delight.

A Mosaic of Reflections

In a world of waits and stops,
Jigsaw pieces of our dreams,
I look for signs in instant crops,
While time stretches at the seams.

Yesterday I tripped on air,
And laughed till my belly hurt,
Said, 'Tomorrow's full of flair!'
As my plans lie in the dirt.

I ponder purpose at the park,
Where squirrels plot and scheme,
With acorns facetime in the dark,
Revealing life's great meme.

So here's to those we sidestep fast,
In pursuit of our grand quest,
Will we be wise, or just outcast?
A mystery, at best!

The Quiet Between Sounds

In the silence, thoughts collide,
Like socks that never match,
A bated breath, a sniper's guide,
To catch what we might hatch.

Whispers ride the breeze like jokes,
Where punchlines dwell in shade,
We pause, then laugh at lesser folks,
Unraveled dreams we've made.

Fleeting moments dance like flies,
A question—what's the worth?
A tasty pie or silly ties,
As we giggle 'round the earth.

Yet here we sit, a curious lot,
Crafting riddles, bold and sly,
In waiting rooms where thoughts get caught,
Like popcorn in my eye!

Holding the Breath of Tomorrow

I hold my breath in crowded lines,
Dreaming big with tiny plans,
While waiting for the stars to align,
And running from the 'nos' and 'cans.'

Every hiccup, a chance to sway,
Dance in place, a silly sight,
Forgetting why I'm here today,
While pizzas wheel into the night.

I glance at clocks with hungry eyes,
Each tick a tease, a playful try,
'Let's eat cake!' the wise one sighs,
As calendars wave bye-bye!

So here's to tomorrows on the shelf,
Collecting dust like long-lost dreams,
We laugh and twirl, forget ourselves,
In whimsical, dazzling schemes!

The Last Page Left Blank

The final chapter's quite the tease,
A page untouched, no lines to read,
I pause and ponder what life sees,
A blank slate, a dumbfound seed.

With scribbles lurking in my head,
And crumpled notes behind the veil,
I raise my cup with thoughts unsaid,
To toast the chaos of the trail.

Each word we draft, a funky rhyme,
A giggle born from curveball stress,
As puzzled folks, we bide our time,
And laugh ourselves to sweet success.

So here's to endings yet undone,
And jigs we'll dance along the line,
The last page waits, let's have some fun,
With blankness ripe for our design!

The Art of Patient Reflection

In the mirror, I stand tall,
Thinking deep, but not at all.
My brain's a maze, a rubber band,
Bouncing thoughts, that's my grand plan.

Sipping tea, I feel so wise,
While plotting moves, with sleepy eyes.
I seek meaning in my snack,
The chocolate chips—they've got my back.

A journey starts from the fridge door,
Yet here I am, just asking for more.
With bags of chips, I take a seat,
And realize, I'm kind of beat.

So here I ponder like a pro,
Between the bites, slow like a tortoise, you know?
I sigh and smile, embrace the chill,
In every pause, there's magic still.

Captured in Every Inhale

Breathing in, I glance around,
Wondering what joy can be found.
A dust bunny rolls across the floor,
'Is my soul in there?' I want to explore.

With every puff, a cloud of thoughts,
Existential questions and random knots.
Inhale, exhale, a dance so sweet,
Like juggling donuts—oh, what a treat!

I try to meditate, find some peace,
But snacks distract me, oh, what a feast!
Fortune cookies whisper in my ear,
"Just eat dessert, have no fear!"

So here I sit, in fragrant bliss,
These moments pause, can't be amiss.
Captured breaths in a comical way,
I giggle as I waste the day.

Waiting for the Dawn

In the twilight, I wait and stare,
The birds sleep tight without a care.
Count the stars? Oh, what a chore,
Do I need a nap? I think I'll snore.

The sun's a sloth, it takes its time,
But I've got snacks, so that's just fine.
Why rush the dawn? It's not so dire,
Especially when coffee's my only fire.

My dreams parade like weird parades,
As crickets play, the night charades.
Patience is key, or so they say,
But I'm just here, dreaming my day away.

So I'll embrace this sleepy wait,
With whimsy thoughts that feel so great.
When dawn arrives, my heart will sing,
But for now, I've got time to bring!

The Space Between Stars

In the vastness of cosmic chatter,
My thoughts drift wild, it's pure platter.
Planets spin, well, look at that!
While I'm still here, just petting the cat.

The space between is quite the mess,
Like a fridge full of leftovers, I must confess.
Dreams collide with food from last week,
Finding purpose in every stale peak.

Constellations spark a giggle or two,
As I ponder deep, with much ado.
But really, who needs all that noise?
When I've got my snacks and silly toys.

So here I float, a celestial clown,
In this weird universe, I'll wear my crown.
Spaces between, full of delight,
I'll just stay here, until it feels right.

Petals Against the Wind

Dancing petals spin with grace,
Caught in gusts, they find their place.
One shouts, 'Hey! I'm going back!'
The others giggle, 'Not quite, Jack!'

A flower thought it had a plan,
But found it's just a luckless fan.
'Round and 'round in wild ballet,
Who knew a breeze could lead astray?

They giggle as they twirl around,
On currents where they are unbound.
One petal sighed, 'I'm tired too.'
Another laughed, 'Let's pause the blue!'

Amidst the dance, they find their cheer,
No need for goals, they have no fear.
As long as laughter fills the air,
Who cares if they're going nowhere?

Sojourn of the Unsure

With choices laid on wobbly shelves,
Decisions made by clueless elves.
One thinks he's found a shiny path,
But trips on dreams and feels the wrath.

A wanderer, lost and in doubt,
Consults the stars, then spins about.
'Should I go left, or is it right?'
The moon just chuckles at the sight.

'Maybe I'll just sit for a while,'
He mutters softly, with a smile.
A squirrel passes with a nut,
While he debates, all in a rut.

In this pause, he sips on time,
Collects lost thoughts, a jumbled rhyme.
Each meandering moment he finds,
Is bursting with the peace it unwinds.

Glimpses of Color in Grey

In a world that's dull and grey,
A splash of paint comes out to play.
One drop rolls down a sidewalk crack,
Whispers, 'Shall I ask the sky back?'

Blues and pinks, like chattering birds,
In corners hiding, spreading words.
'C'mon, don't let the dreariness win!'
They splutter laughter, shake and grin.

Puddles gleam with colors bright,
Reflecting joys in the fading light.
With messy brush strokes that don't conform,
They giggle, 'Art redefined the norm!'

So here's to those bright flecks of cheer,
Living entrees in a banquet of drear.
Each moment swirls with comic flair,
In our monochrome, let's paint the air!

Voices at the Edge of Tomorrow

Whispers echo from the unknown,
Stitching futures with threads of tone.
'Tomorrow's just a silly charade,'
Said one, while the other's fears displayed.

'Should we dive or take it slow?'
The cautious one, feeling the flow.
'Let's send postcards to yesterday!'
With pen in hand, they joke and sway.

The edge is tight, a comical stage,
Where laughter dances, uncaged from age.
'We could fly or simply fall,'
Said the dreamer with hopes tall.

They pause a moment, to sigh and jest,
'What if we just took a rest?'
And before they leap, the fun begins,
A friendship forged, as laughter spins!

Echoes of Intent

I planned to climb the highest peak,
But tripped on socks, oh what a week.
My goals, they glittered, oh so bright,
Now I nap till noon, that feels just right.

A thousand dreams, I let them fleet,
Chasing butterflies, oh isn't that sweet?
My vision board, has turned to art,
Of doodles made with an idle heart.

I shout to stars, with chocolate bars,
While pondering life beneath my stars.
My to-do list is by now quite huge,
Yet here I sit, sipping sweet fruit juice.

Maybe one day I'll redefine,
These wacky thoughts that snugly entwine.
But for now, I'll enjoy this ride,
And let my dreams just slide, slide, slide.

In the Quiet Moment

In splendid stillness, I sit and stare,
At dust bunnies, floating midair.
Plans I once had, now softly rest,
In the embrace of this lazy quest.

My dreams sit stacked, like old magazines,
But here with snacks, life's pretty keen.
I'm told to hustle, but I just yawn,
I'll catch my thrills in the early dawn.

I once was fierce, a seeker bold,
Now I snack while stories unfold.
The universe laughs with a gentle nudge,
As I plot my path from the comfort of fudge.

Perhaps tomorrow, I'll rise and dance,
But wait, there's popcorn! I'll just take a chance.
For now, I'll giggle through these bemused plots,
Filling my world with laughter and thoughts.

A Journey on Hold

Packed my bags for great escapes,
But forgot how to tie my shoelace shapes.
The map is lost, but hey, that's cool,
I'll explore the fridge, that's my new rule.

Adventure calls, or so they say,
From comfy chairs, who needs the fray?
I'm Robin Hood, stealing snacks with glee,
In this epic quest called couchery.

The world awaits; my smartphone dings,
But lemurs and I are doing funny things.
From browsing memes to loopy songs,
This stillness hums where my heart belongs.

Tomorrow's sunrise might bring my stride,
But for today, I'll enjoy this ride.
Maybe I'll wander, but not just yet,
An adventure paused is not a regret.

Reflections in Limbo

In wobbly mirrors, I strike a pose,
Who knew my ambition wears silly clothes?
Reflection jokes, they come alive,
In the world where sloths can thrive.

I ponder plans from yesterday's dream,
But my coffee mug has more esteem.
Goals like balloons float high, oh why?
I'll major in laughter, give that a try.

Staring at ceilings, ideas float through,
Counted sheep turn to people in blue.
Thoughts of grandeur, I'll push aside,
While ice cream sundaes become my guide.

As echoes of laughter bounce off the wall,
I sit uncooked, not worried at all.
In moments of pause, I dance on my own,
Creating a universe nobody's known.

The Land of Almost

In the Land of Almost, dreams do roam,
Where socks lose their pairs and Wi-Fi's a comb.
I start to run errands but end up in bed,
With ice cream and shows filling up my head.

The fridge is my best friend, we share all we can,
While laundry piles high, I just don't understand.
The world keeps on spinning, yet I pause to stare,
At cat videos on loop that fill the air.

I almost found purpose while lounging around,
But the couch had its plans, it trapped me, I found.
With each little snack, my ambitions do fade,
In this land of "almost," I'm not too dismayed!

So cheers to the chaos, the fun, and the laugh,
In the Land of Almost, I'll just take a bath.
With bubbles and giggles, my goals take a break,
In a world made of dreams, it's all mine to make!

A Thread Unspooled

A thread unspooled leads me here and there,
Like a knitting disaster with no one to care.
I thought I was wise, full of plans, big and grand,
But I trip on the yarn, and oh, how I've planned!

The patterns are tangled, my needles are lost,
Yet I chase after laughter, I don't count the cost.
In a whirl of confusion, I spin and I twirl,
While the cats have conspired, their plan's in a swirl.

I almost made progress and crafted a dream,
But the thread's tangled up, or so it would seem.
If I measure my joy by stitches I weave,
Then I'm oh so successful, just watch me believe!

So pass me the scissors, let chaos restore,
In a world that's unraveled, I simply want more.
For life's all about laughs, even when a thread frays,
And the fun's in each moment, come what may!

The Perils of Uncharted

In the perils of uncharted, I set the course,
With maps made of pizza and a strong source of force.
The to-do list is rising, but oh, who can tell,
When the world's an adventure, and I'm under its spell?

With a spatula in hand, I set sail in the kitchen,
Where recipes blend and the smoke alarms chirpin'.
I chart out great dishes, vivid and bright,
But the takeout's delicious and just feels so right!

I brave the wild grocery aisles, armor of carts,
But one wrong turn leads to chaos in parts.
With visions of cooking, I gather my loot,
Only to realize, I don't own a fruit!

So here in this adventure, I laugh and I sway,
In the perils of uncharted, I'll find my way.
With humor as treasure and joy as my sound,
In a world unexplored, my heart's unbound!

Quietude of the Heart

In the quietude of the heart, I search for a snack,
Like a squirrel on a mission, I've got a whole pack.
With cookies and chips, serenading my soul,
In moments of stillness, I lose all control.

I meditate deeply, embrace all the Zen,
But then I spy brownies, and oh, there and then!
The calm turns to chaos, I toss out the plan,
As the quietude giggles, it really knows how to span.

In stillness, I ponder the depths of my dreams,
But is it a chocolate? Or cheese? It redeems.
On this path to enlightenment, I take a reprieve,
With whispers of laughter, I don't want to leave.

The heart's a fun rogue, it dances and feasts,
Finding joy in the simple, where worry just ceased.
So here's to the quiet, with giggles that dart,
In the stillness, we flourished, sweet snack to the heart!

The Crucible of Choices

In the kitchen, pots collide,
My dinner plans hang on a tide.
Should it be pasta or heaping rice?
I'll just order takeout—what's nice?

The laundry pile stares, it won't flee,
Stains whisper secrets like me.
Match the socks? That's just too much.
I'll set them free—what's the rush?

Weekend plans are all a-hooey,
Can't find my keys, feeling a bit gooey.
In this dance of mishaps and flops,
I'll raise a toast with a soda pops!

So as I wander this winding way,
Juggling tasks like a circus display.
Who knew choices could bamboozle so?
Let's just laugh and let the chaos flow!

Surrender to the Pause

Clicking 'snooze' feels so divine,
The day can wait, it's clearly fine.
Dreams of work swirl in my head,
But pillows whisper, 'Stay in bed!'

Gather my thoughts, like cats on a spree,
Chasing their tails, they giggle with glee.
'Productivity's overrated,' they say,
But Netflix's 'next episode' calls me away!

Is it really 'me time' if I nap?
With snacks piled high on my lap.
Each bite's a treasure from the fridge,
On this rollercoaster, I'm the smidge!

So let's embrace this funny game,
Where pause is king, and stress is lame.
In the grand scheme, what's the rush?
Let laughter lead, in silence, we hush!

Contexts of the Heart

Oh, relationships in a swirl,
Like spaghetti tossed in a whirl.
Do I like him, or just his snacks?
Heart's in a tangle, cut out the hacks!

Texting emojis to express my feels,
Each heart or wink—am I keeping it real?
Over-analyzing every line,
Just send a GIF, and all will be fine!

Friendship's a dance, but I've got two left,
Tripping on jokes where laughter's the theft.
Can we mute worries, just for a while?
Dancing through life with a quirky smile!

So let's toast to hearts in jest,
Crafting our lives with humor—no less.
In this circus of love, we play our part,
Twisting and turning in the contexts of heart!

Hushed Anticipation

Eagerly waiting for the mail to arrive,
To see if my package will come alive.
Each knock on the door is a mini thrill,
It's just the neighbor? Well, that's a skill!

The clock ticks as I brew my tea,
Wondering if it'll be fun to be me.
Days stretch longer than a yawning cat,
With hopes and fancies, where's the spat?

A surprise? Oh please, let it be bright!
Maybe a llama or a disco ball light?
The universe grins, whispering fun,
With every pause, the adventure's begun!

So here's to the wait for what's not yet known,
Embracing the absurdity I've blown.
In this quiet space, possibilities dance,
Life's just a jest, let's seize our chance!

A Garden in the Shade

In a garden where daisies play,
I ponder what to do today.
Should I nap or chase a bug?
My motives stretch like a cozy rug.

The sun's high, but I'm feeling low,
Should I dance or put on a show?
Instead, I'll sip my lemonade,
While pondering adventures I've low-key made.

With weeds that whisper, 'Grow with ease,'
I think I'll lounge beneath the trees.
The squirrels laugh; they've got it right,
While I'm just trying to avoid the light.

So here I sit, while time is galloping,
With a voice in my head, that's just babbling—
"Do something grand!" it shouts with glee,
Yet I just smile, "Maybe later...or maybe me!"

The Art of Lingering

The clock ticks slow, a tortoise's race,
Yet here I lounge, an indolent ace.
Should I rise? I glance at the floor,
But the couch calls me, 'Just a bit more.'

My thoughts drift like clouds in the breeze,
Wondering what snacks I'll forage with ease.
Should I bake cookies or simply snack?
I choose the sofa, no need to track.

I feel like a pro at procrastination,
Creating an art form of this situation.
With cartoons playing and coffee in hand,
My grand plans go drifting to a distant land.

As the daylight fades into evening's glow,
I think of adventures I'll never bestow.
Yet, in all my lounging, I find a delight,
In the art of just being, it feels so right!

A Time to Savor

Morning coffee, a sip to ponder,
Chocolate croissants—a divine fonder.
Do I work or do I graze?
Savoring snacks through a delicious haze.

Time wears a stretchy pair of pants,
While I dance in the kitchen, giving cupcakes a chance.
Should I bake or eat what's in sight?
My apron's on, so tonight's a delight!

Minutes turn to hours, oh what a feat,
While I'm caught in a loop of something sweet.
Shall I go out or embrace inside?
An inner voice says, 'A cozy ride.'

Savoring moments, both funny and quaint,
Avoiding the hustle, feeling like a saint.
In this sweet chaos, I twirl and I spin,
Finding joy in the now, let the savoring begin!

The Thickness of Dreams

Dreams thick as pudding, a sweet delight,
I am flying high, what a curious sight.
Should I chase them or let them be?
They giggle and dance, while I sip my tea.

But wait! Reality knocks on the door,
Saying, 'Get up, stop dreaming, there's much to explore.'
Yet here I stay, with my head in the clouds,
Laughing at worries, ignoring the crowds.

With ambitions as big as a giant's shoe,
I wonder if they still fit; do they work for you?
Yet I'll take a moment, let the thick dreams flow,
Like a lazy river where I won't have to go.

So I feign an effort with a yawn and a stretch,
While dreams gently tug, like a softest wretch.
This pause is quite nice, no need to speed,
In the thickness of dreams, I'll plant my seed.

Waiting for the Muse

I sit with coffee in my hand,
As ideas dance, just out of hand.
A cat walks by, gives me a stare,
I wonder if she knows I care.

The clock ticks on, a mocking sound,
Inspiration lost, nowhere to be found.
I check my phone, nothing new,
Just memes and cats – all the things I rue.

A sock awaits its partner's grace,
While I'm stuck in this mindless race.
I scribble down a weird new thought,
Should I write? Oh wait, I'm still caught!

The day drips by, like melted cheese,
Where's my spark? Oh, hold the keys.
I search for meaning in a bowl of dough,
But laughter's voice says, "Just let it flow!"

A Flicker in the Fog

Amid the mist, my thoughts are lost,
I fumble round, not caring the cost.
A seagull squawks, gives me a fright,
Yet I laugh out loud at this crazy sight.

Clouds roll in, my brain's on strike,
Is it me, or just my bike?
Wheels are turning, but going slow,
Guess my dreams are all on hold.

I chase ideas like a kid with a kite,
But winds are calm; there's no flight tonight.
My calendar laughs, "You're a funny guy!"
I laugh back, "Well, at least I try!"

Foggy nights turn to morning light,
With every giggle, wrong feels right.
Days may muddle; paths might switch,
But hey, who says we're in a glitch?

Reflections of What Could Be

In the mirror, I see a face,
Half asleep, lost in space.
I tell myself, "Hey, here's the deal,
We ponder hard; we'll spin the wheel."

Thoughts parade like a circus train,
Juggling dreams and a sprinkle of pain.
A peek at futures, like candy in jars,
Each taste takes me to distant stars.

I wish on wishes, oh what a bore,
Each wish comes back, knocking at the door.
I could be great, or so I'm told,
But first, let's find the remote to hold!

I muse on paths just out of reach,
While my cat comes in, a wise old screech.
"Your dreams are dreams unless you leap;
Now feed me, please, I need my sleep!"

Echoes of Unspoken Desires

In the garden of hopes, I plant my thoughts,
Water them gently, like cherished spots.
But weeds grow wild, with a twist and twine,
Who would've guessed they were all by design?

I shout to the wind, "What's your grand plan?"
The breeze just laughs, "Son, you're the man!"
Every whisper of wish drifts back to me,
Returning with giggles, oh how carefree!

I ponder on pathways, like roads made of gold,
Yet here I am, feeling quite old.
An echo of laughter fills up the air,
As I chase down dreams with not much to bear.

With each unspoken, my heart takes flight,
Spin me around in this dance of light.
Like a clown on a stage, I'll juggle and grin,
Perhaps my desires enjoy the din!

Chasing Half-Voiced Wishes

In the garden of dreams, we play,
Catching shadows that run away.
Whispers linger, mischief in air,
But all we find is a broken chair.

Socks mismatched, like thoughts in a whirl,
Chasing after the next great twirl.
With each bounce, we ponder our goal,
Yet trip on the dreams that beguile our soul.

Laughter echoes in the late afternoon,
While we dance to a satirical tune.
We shake hands with time, a clumsy affair,
And wonder if wishes will ever get there.

As we stand by the pond's quirky gate,
Frogs croak wisdom we often berate.
"Leap with us!" they quip with a grin,
While we fumble for the start of our spin.

Beneath the Surface of Now

In a bubble of thought, I drift and sway,
Trying to find what words won't say.
Beneath the surface, it's all just foam,
Where fleeting ideas forget to roam.

Milking the cows of my mind's own field,
Where grazing ideas refuse to yield.
They chew on the thoughts, then burst like a bubble,
Leaving behind a perplexing muddle.

I sit on the couch, remote in hand,
Watching reruns in a dishwater land.
Schedules slip like jello from plates,
As I ponder the quirks of my fates.

Here in the now, everything's bizarre,
Chasing half thoughts in a candy bar.
Who knew existence could be this fun?
A game of hide and seek with no one!

A Train Station of the Heart

At the station where dreams come to rest,
Trains full of hopes go west and then jest.
Platforms of feelings await the next ride,
As passengers ponder if joy's inside.

Tickets in hand, but lost at the gate,
They giggle aloud at their twist of fate.
The train whistling loud seems too far away,
While I juggle my thoughts and a pine-scented spray.

Baggage of memories slips from my grip,
As I spill my secrets, where giggles trip.
The conductor just winks, "What's your next stop?"
And I shrug my shoulders while soda pop hops.

But off goes the train with a heartily cheer,
Leaving behind all my laughter and fear.
Here's to delays, and a life somewhat weird,
Where the arrival time's just what we feared.

When Paths Cross and Fade

Two paths diverged with a clumsy flip,
We walked hand in hand, gave laughter a lip.
Then a blender of choices blended our fate,
And suddenly dinner seemed a bit late.

Once we danced on the edge of a dare,
Eating cotton candy, without a care.
Now we pause at the crosswalk of fate,
With shoes untied and a snack that's first-rate.

The world's spinning fast, like a roller coaster,
With each twist and turn, we're why I'm the poster.
But who knew the map had a sense of the jest?
As we search for the humor in every quest.

When paths cross and fade, we giggle anew,
In a dance with the cosmos, where daydreams brew.
We toss out our worries like breadcrumbs in air,
And take crazy flights on a whim without care.

A Haven of Uncertainty

In the land of 'Maybe', I roam all day,
Wearing mismatched socks, it's just my way.
The calendar's blank, my plans in a mess,
Yet I'd trade all my chaos for a moment of rest.

With cereal for dinner, and movies at noon,
I dance with the dust bunnies, to my own tune.
The fridge is a puzzle, what treats lie inside?
A mystery unfolds where leftovers hide!

Fragments of What Lies Ahead

I stared at my future, it waved back at me,
With a wink and a grin, it said, "Just wait and see!"
I scribble my dreams on napkins and walls,
As fortune cookies giggle with their cryptic calls.

Each step feels like juggling while riding a bike,
The slightest misstep? Oh, what a life hike!
Yet laughter's my compass, it points the right way,
To a treasure of giggles in the light of the day.

A Solace of the Unsung

They say I'm a poet— I guess that's the vibe,
Though my rhymes are more sticky than honey on a bribe.
I take life's little hiccups, turn them into gold,
In my circus of wonders, I'm forever enrolled.

The clock ticks away, but I'm lost in my thoughts,
Like a cat lost in yarn, a web of unknots.
There's joy in the chaos, a smile in the fray,
Even socks in the dryer are learning to play!

Beyond the Crossroads

Here I stand at the fork, where to go, I can't tell,
One road leads to coffee, the other to a shell.
Flip a coin or just dance under whimsical stars,
My compass is broken, but hey, that's a plus!

If a snail can travel, then surely I might,
To a land where the mornings are always polite.
With humor my guide, I'll wander awhile,
Searching for joy in a world full of trial.

Hushed Resilience

In pajamas that cling like a second skin,
I ponder the zest of where I have been.
The fridge calls to me, a siren so sweet,
As I waddle around for my next snack to greet.

The couch is my throne, the remote my crown,
In a kingdom of cushions, I wear my renown.
I sip from my mug, filled with questionable brews,
And laugh at the moments life seemed to lose.

Outside the window, the world's in a rush,
But here, in my castle, there's never a hush.
My to-do list is dusty, neglected like me,
Yet I bask in the pause, so blissfully free.

If I stumble upon a lost sock or two,
I'll champion my quest, for that's what I do.
In this playful interlude where time takes a break,
I find joy in the silly, my own little quake.

Threads of Anticipation

As I sit with a snack, contemplating the sky,
I'm strung up on hopes like a kite way up high.
The laundry's a monster, a mountain untamed,\nYet I lie
on the couch, and I can't feel ashamed.

I've got dreams piled high like my tower of clothes,
With a spritz of ambition that sometimes just slows.
My goals float around like balloons in thin air,
And I chuckle out loud at my whimsical dare.

The clock ticks away like a metronome slow,
In this circus of life, I'm a star in the show.
With a laugh and a wink, but still no great plan,
I take each day lightly, as best as I can.

So here's to the moments, both silly and grand,
To dwelling in pauses with snacks close at hand.
I'll keep writing this story, one chuckle at a time,
In the tapestry woven of laughter and rhyme.

A Breath Between Dreams

I drift on the couch, a nautical breeze,
With snacks in my lap, floating in a tease.
The dreams that I chase seem to flutter and dance,
While I nap for a while, giving fate a fair chance.

Between broken rhythms of errands unkept,
I ponder the secrets while napping and swept.
With each little snooze, new ideas may bloom,
So I'll rest here forever in my cozy cocoon.

The world feels so distant, like a muffled song,
While I linger at home where I truly belong.
And when evening arrives, I'll rise with a grin,
Blessed by this pause where the laughter begins.

I'll embrace all the quirks in life's wobbly seam,
Finding joy in the gaps, stitching seams with a dream.
For amid all the chaos of what I might miss,
I'll take this sweet breath, it's a simple bliss.

The Stillness of Now

In the stillness of now, the world takes a breather,
I snuggle my blanket like a warm pizza pleather.
The TV flickers on, a poor substitute friend,
But here in this moment, I don't want it to end.

The cat sprawls beside me, a regal delight,
While I sip on my coffee that's slightly too light.
Plans swirl in my head like confetti on air,
But my fingers are glued to this plush, furry lair.

From the depths of the couch, I ponder my fate,
In the stillness I find, I embrace the mundane rate.
With laughter and giggles that sprinkle the hours,
I remember that purpose comes dressed in soft flowers.

So let the world whirl, and let time slip away,
I'm basking in moments that twist and sway.
For joy often hides in the simplest ways,
In the stillness of now, life's surprises stay.

An Idle Compass

A compass spins with glee,
Chasing after cup of tea.
It points to nothing, just a laugh,
A treasure map? Just a giraffe!

The North is where I want to play,
But all I find is Mr. Gray.
His cat insists on more fun games,
Like hide and seek with silly names.

The East is where I'd bake a pie,
But all I get is a sigh and fry.
A donut's path, a frosty breeze,
My aim is off, like missing keys.

Each direction holds a riddle sweet,
But wandering's more fun than a treat.
With laughter light and jokes that sail,
This idle compass will not fail!

Yearning in Still Waters

In ponds where ducklings drift and sway,
I sit and ponder where to play.
The ripples tease, they giggle slight,
While boats whirl round like kites in flight.

I yearn for shores, but here I stay,
Trapped in thoughts that dance and sway.
The fish make jokes, they shimmer bright,
While I just float, an awkward sight.

A frog croaks tales of skies so vast,
But here I sit, a boredom blast.
I dream of sails, of winds that sing,
Yet listless here, I'm just a thing!

In still waters, the laughter flows,
With turtles pondering where it goes.
Though yearning twirls around my frame,
I chuckle loud, it's all a game!

The Pensive Journey

A journey starts with sock-less shoes,
With thoughts that scatter like the blues.
A ponder here, a ponder there,
What if the world is just a fair?

With every step I trip and fall,
A laughing ghost shouts, 'Not at all!'
My mind spins round like dizzy pins,
A carnival of deep chagrins.

The road is paved with silly signs,
Turn back, they say, but where's the fun?
So onward goes my clumsy quest,
Seeking wisdom, what a jest!

In pondering paths and routes unseen,
The pencil skids, it's not too keen.
But joy resides where head meets ground,
In thoughtless laughs, the truth is found!

Gathering Flickers of Light

A jar awaits for fireflies bright,
To catch their giggles, soft as night.
I wave my arms, they skitter past,
Their dances tease my clumsy grasp.

In garden nights, they twinkle so,
Yet all I catch is leaves below.
A flicker here, a jiggle there,
It feels like dancing in midair!

I gather dreams like buzzing bees,
Hoping just one will be at ease.
While critters laugh from tree to tree,
My jar stays empty, oh woe is me!

Yet in the chase with power moves,
I find a joy that bubbles, grooves.
For in the folly, glimmers gleam,
It's not the jar, but fun's the theme!

The Interlude of Intent

With coffee in hand, I sit and stare,
Dreams on the shelf, do I even care?
The clock ticks slow, like molasses in fall,
What was my goal? I can't recall!

A squirrel outside takes a wild leap,
While I'm deciding if I need more sleep.
Sandwiches, naps, and the occasional dance,
My plans have turned into a sitcom chance!

Is it too late to become a rock star?
I'll hum in the shower and practice guitar.
The world spins on with its grand parade,
While I'm here pondering how, when, and made.

So here's to the pause, the lull in the race,
To belly laughs and a slower pace.
When life gives you lemons, make lemon meringue,
I'll just chill here while the universe hangs.

A Journey on Hold

Packed my bags, thought I'd take flight,
But Netflix called, it felt so right!
Adventure awaits, or so they claim,
Yet here I am, playing the binge-watch game.

Maps and plans are cluttering the floor,
While I contemplate snacks and maybe more.
The open road doesn't seem so bright,
When a hefty burger is in my sight.

I could be out there chasing the sun,
Instead, I'm chasing down a devilish bun.
With each episode, my dreams take a pause,
Lost in the plot, ignoring all calls.

Yet maybe these moments are part of the fun,
As I ponder what could be under this sun.
The journey awaits, I'll get there someday,
But for now, I'll just laugh as I stay.

Shadows of What Could Be

In dreams I dance on a twinkling shore,
But reality says, 'Not right now, poor.'
I try to leap, but my feet are bound,
To the couch where my ambition's drowned.

Shadows of grandeur float through my head,
While I trade them for chips and soft bread.
So I stash my cape and superhero cape,
For a night of re-runs that don't need escape.

What if tomorrow I rise with the sun?
Only if there's coffee—I'll have some fun!
Or should I just lay here and dream of flight,
While sipping on lattes with all of my might?

And who knows, maybe soon I'll be bold,
Though my quest is on ice, and the world feels cold.
I'll laugh at the shadows and toss in a grin,
For the adventures that wait, they just might begin!

The Unturned Page

There's a book on my shelf, dust thick as clay,
One day I'll read it, I promise, okay?
The cover looks thrilling, really, it should,
But let's be real, it's misunderstood!

I promised myself that I'd turn the next leaf,
Yet here I am, stuck in my coffee grief.
With chapters unwritten, and plots rather sly,
I'd rather deep dive in a pie as I sigh.

The characters dance in their paper cage,
While I sit in my chair, full of indigence rage.
But laughs can be found in this stifling wait,
As I ponder what wonders might come from fate.

So here's to the stories I perhaps will dare,
To explore them or not, in a grand, wild affair.
Until then, I'll chuckle at joys to engage,
As I postpone each marvelous, unturned page!

www.ingramcontent.com/pod-product-compliance
Lightning Source LLC
Chambersburg PA
CBHW051650160426
43209CB00004B/855